# How to Get Better at Decision Making

## A Step by Step Guide to Effective Decision Making Techniques

I0462851

## By Meir Liraz

Published by BizMove
www.bizmove.com

# Table of Contents

MEIR LIRAZ

# 1. Introduction

Everyone is a decision maker. We all rely on information, and techniques or tools, to help us in our daily lives. When we go out to eat, the restaurant menu is the tool that provides us with the information needed to decide what to purchase and how much to spend. Operating a business also requires making decisions using information and techniques - how much inventory to maintain, what price to sell it at, what credit arrangements to offer, how many people to hire.

Decision making in business is the systematic process of identifying and solving problems, of asking questions and finding answers. Decisions usually are made under conditions of uncertainty. The future is not known and sometimes even the past is suspect. This guide opens the door for business owners and managers to learn about the variety of techniques which can be used to improve decision making in a world of uncertainty, change, and uncontrollable circumstances.

## 2. A General Approach to Decision Making

Whether a scientist, an executive of a major corporation, or a small business owner, the general approach to systematically solving problems is the same. The following 7 step approach to better management decision making can be used to study nearly all problems faced by a business.

### 1. State the problem

A problem first must exist and be recognized. What is the problem and why is it a problem. What is ideal and how do current operations vary from that ideal. Identify why the symptoms (what is going wrong) and the causes (why is it going wrong). Try to define all terms, concepts, variables, and relationships. Quantify the problem to the extent possible. If the problem, not accurately and quickly filling customer orders, try to determine how many orders were incorrectly filled and how long it took to fill them.

### 2. Define the Objectives

What are the objectives of the study. Which objectives are the most critical. Objectives usually are stated by an action verb like to reduce, to increase, or to improve. Returning to the customer order problem, the major objectives would be: 1) to increase the percentage of orders filled correctly, and 2) to reduce the time it takes to process and order. A subobjective could include to simplify and streamline the order filling process.

## 3. Develop a Diagnostic Framework

Next establish a diagnostic framework, that is, decide what methods are going to be used, what kinds of information are needed, and how and where the information is to be found. Is there going to be a customer survey, a review of company documents, time and motion tests, or something else. What are the assumptions (facts assumed to be correct) of the study. What are the criteria used to judge the study. What time, budget, or other constraints are there. What kind of quantitative or other specific techniques are going to be used to analyze the data. (Some of which will be covered shortly). In other words, the diagnostic framework establishes the scope and methods of the entire study.

## 4. Collect and Analyze the Data

The next step is to collect the data (by following the

methods established in Step 3. Raw data is then tabulated and organized to facilitate analysis. Tables, charts, graphs, indexes and matrices are some of the standard ways to organize raw data. Analysis is the critical prerequisite of sound business decision making. What does the data reveal. What facts, patterns, and trends can be seen in the data. Many of the quantitative techniques covered below can be used during the step to determine facts, patterns, and trends in data. Of course, computers are used extensively during this step.

## 5. Generate Alternative Solutions

After the analysis has been finished, some specific conclusions about the nature of the problem and its resolution should have been reached. The next step is to develop alternative solutions to the problem and rank them in order of their net benefits. But how are alternatives best generated. Again, there are several well established techniques such as the Nominal Group Method, the Delphi Method and Brainstorming, among others. In all these methods a group is involved, all of whom have reviewed the data and analysis. The approach is to have an informed group suggesting a variety of possible solutions.

## 6. Develop an Action Plan and Implement

Select the best solution to the problem but be certain to understand clearly why it is best, that is, how it achieves the objectives established in Step 2 better than its alternatives. Then develop an effective method (Action Plan) to implement the solution. At this point an important organizational consideration arises - who is going to be responsible for seeing the implementation through and what authority does he have. The selected manager should be responsible for seeing that all tasks, deadlines, and reports are performed, met, and written. Details are important in this step: schedules, reports, tasks, and communication are the key elements of any action plan. There are several techniques available to decision makers implementing an action plan. The PERT method is a way of laying out an entire period such as an action plan. PERT will be covered shortly.

## 7. Evaluate, obtain Feedback and Monitor

After the Action Plan has been implemented to solve a problem, management must evaluate its effectiveness. Evaluation standards must be determined, feedback channels developed, and monitoring performed. This Step should be done after 3 to 5 weeks and again at 6 months. The goal is to answer the bottom line question. Has the problem been solved?

# 3. Specific Decision Making Techniques

The following techniques are used frequently by business and government managers. Some are familiar (Benefit-Cost Analysis), others more esoteric (Linear Programming). Some are used for planning projects, others for analyzing data. Most of these techniques are mathematical or have mathematical aspects to them. They all can be used during one or more of the steps of he General Approach, as just outlined.

## Systems Analysis

Can be used by the business manager to study the inputs, processes, and outputs of the entire company, a division, or an office, depending on the nature of the problem. Inputs are the resources (manpower, materials, facilities) used by the business to produce the output (goods or services). Processes are the methods and organization which manager the conversion of inputs to outputs. By using Systems Analysis decision makers can evaluate the system's various components separately on the basis of established objectives (like cost or error rate). If a problem can be identified as belonging to a specific component of the system, it can be corrected.

## Benefit-Cost Analysis

Is used to compare the pros and cons of various alternative solutions to a problem. To perform this type of analysis the manager must define the problem, determine objectives, develop alternatives, put a dollar value on all benefits and costs of each alternative, calculate the Benefit Cost Ratio (B divided by C) and/or the Net Benefit (B-C), and make the decision. This type analysis established a clear relationship between expenditure (cost) and purchase (benefit). It can be used to study problems in which the costs and benefits of alternative ways to achieve an objective can be assigned dollar values.

## Input-Output Analysis

Charts the flow of a product from one industrial sector, company, department, or facility to another. It shows what inputs produce what outputs. I/O Analysis uses Transaction Tables, showing the purchasing and selling activities of buyers and sellers, and I/O Coefficients, the product sold by A to B divided by the output of B. It is used most often by larger companies to help with longer term planning but smaller manufacturing firms also may find this useful.

## Regression and Correlation Analysis

Is used to study the relationship between or among variables, for example, the relationship of household income to product sales. It can be used to determine how increases in household income affect sales volume. If management wants to study the relationship between sales, and income, interest rates, and education, they would use Multiple Regression Analysis, Correlation Analysis refers to the study of how strong or accurate a relationship is, as well as such technical factors as measurement fit, deviation, and error. It often is used by companies to study demand, pricing, supply and cost curves.

## Modeling

Is used by management to simplify the complex world. A model is a (simplified) representation of a system, situation, or process. A model may be physical, symbolic, verbal, graphic, or mathematical. A good model strips away excess detail but leaves essential behavior. For example, a model could be a representation of a distribution system illustrated graphically with a flow chart. Models show relationships among the parts of a whole and assist with forecasting. Model building is used in the physical and social sciences, as well as in business management.

## Linear Programming

Is a widely used mathematical method of determining an optimum, single solution to a problem such as finding the minimum staff cost or the most nutritional mixture of ingredients. This technique can be done by hand but today's computer software business management packages often contain Linear Programming instructions. The technique can only be used with problems that can be translated entirely into numbers and have with a single, optimum objective or solution. For example, in an office situation (say processing invoices) where there is a given total workload, an established workload per worker by skill (pay) level, and given staffing requirements, linear programming could be used to determine the least expensive mixture of worker skill levels to handle the given workload.

## Econometric Analysis

Is used by companies (and the Government) for planning, forecasting, and model building. Through this type of analysis businesses can estimate demand cycles, cost and supply functions, income distribution changes, and so forth. Econometrics uses regression and correlation analysis. It is an attempt to quantify as many variables affecting a business as is possible. Larger companies often develop econometric models to get a picture of the future economy.

## Forecasting

Is making decisions based on predictions of future trends and events such as inflation and interest rates, employment levels, or supply costs - all of which can affect sales of small businesses. There are three types of forecasting techniques: 1) Subjective or qualitative where you rely on expert judgments, 2) Time-Series Projections where you use quantifiable observations over time, and 3) Casual Models where you emphasize causal/correlational relationships. The principal emphasis in forecasting is looking for patterns and fluctuations over time.

## The Decision Tree

Technique plots the sequence of alternative decisions needed to solve a larger problem. The actual decision tree looks like a flow chart. Each alternative decision has consequences that lead to other decisions. These are all drawn as branches of the tree. One can also add probability and payoff calculations for each decision. The major feature of the Decision Tree technique is that solutions to a complex problem can be sketched out on a single sheet of paper.

## PERT - Program Evaluation and Review Technique

Sequentially charts the individual tasks and activities needed to complete a project. The result is a flow chart of the entire job. A time schedule and probabilities of meeting that schedule can be plugged in. The Critical Path also can be determined (the longest time it will take to complete all the important tasks, which gives the completion date). PERT helps managers make decisions about scheduling and resource allocation and reduces uncertainty. PERT is often used on construction projects and was pioneered by Admiral Rickover when he ran the Nation's nuclear submarine production program. However, PERT is a very flexible tool and also can be used, for example, to do market research.

# Bonus Guide

## 4. How To Set and Achieve Goals

Life is a journey. Not just any journey, but the most fantastic journey in the universe. Life is a journey from where you are to where you want to be. You can choose your own destination. Not only that, you can choose how you are going to get there. Goal setting will help you end up where you want to be.

-- When it comes to setting goals, start off with what's important to you in life. Take out a sheet of paper. Sit quietly, and on that sheet of paper, brainstorm what you want to accomplish between now and the end of your life.

-- Second step-use another sheet of paper, and this time consider yourself and your personal goals for the next 12 month period. Some key areas in which you might set personal goals include: family, personal growth, financial, health, social, career, hobbies, spiritual, and recreation. Write down the things that you plan to accomplish or achieve or attain during this one-year period?

-- Now, as a third step, go back and compare the

two goal lists you have made. Make sure that the items on your short-term list will, as you attain them, be helping you attain your long-term or lifetime goals. It is important that what you are doing short term is taking you in the right direction toward your lifetime goals. Please rewrite your short term goals now if you need to.

-- As a next step, looking at the goals that are on your list at this time, if there are any that you are not willing to pay the price for, go ahead and cross them out, leaving only those items you are willing to cause to happen in your life. This does not necessarily mean you have the money or the other resources for attaining the goal right now. However, when you do have it, would you spend it on or trade it for the goals you have on your list?

-- Now, on still another sheet of paper, create the job goals that are important to you during this upcoming 12-month period. Identify what outcomes you wish to attain or achieve during this one-year period in your specific area of responsibility and authority.

-- Some key areas in which you might consider writing job goals, if you did not already, include:

quality, quantity, cost control, cost improvement, equipment, procedures, training, sales, financial, and personnel.

-- As a next step, look for the blending between your job or work goals and your personal goals. Anywhere you notice that you are attaining a goal on the job while at the same time you are attaining a personal goal, note this relationship: it is in these areas you will be most highly motivated.

-- For each of the three lists that you have just created, take an additional sheet of paper and list the activities that you must do to attain the most important goal that you have on each of your lists.

-- Now on another piece of paper titled "Things To-Do List" identify from the activities you just listed, the ones that you must do tomorrow to move you toward your most important goal.

-- Rewrite your goals in these categories at least every three months.

-- The only thing in life that is constant is the fact that everything is changing. It makes sense that our goals will change as we change.

-- Recognize how focusing on what you do want,

what you do intend to accomplish, also defines what you choose not to do in your life.

Daily rewrite your list of "Things To-Do" after first reviewing your desired goals.

-- Success is defined as "the progressive realization of a worthwhile goal." If you are doing the things that are moving you toward the attainment of your goal, then you are "successful" even if you are not there yet.

-- Every step along the way to achieving a goal is just as important as the last step.

-- It is not the achieving of a goal that is so important, it is what you become in the process.

-- Set goals with your family also. Help children learn this process early in life.

-- Decide what you should be accomplishing and then stick to your knitting. Do not attempt to be or do all things for all people.

-- Dreams and wishes are not goals until they are written as specific end results on paper.

-- Written specific goals provide direction and focus to your activities. They become a road map to follow.

-- Being busy with activities does not pay, only results do. As in baseball you only get points for getting to the goal of home plate. Just making it to the bases does not count.

-- It has been said that the amount of information available to us is now doubling in less than 30 months. We must learn to focus on only what is truly important to our self and our job.

-- Be sure the goals and activities that you are working for are yours and that you really want and desire to achieve them. The commitment is vital to your success in achieving them.

-- When you have a goal that is exciting to you, the life energy flows through you. You are excited about accomplishing it because it is personally meaningful.

-- Create a time line or matrix chart on which you display your goals visually and the dates when you will have them accomplished.

-- Continually look for ways to integrate or blend personal and professional goals.

-- Setting a goal, that you believe is unattainable will result in frustration. To be challenging and motivating, goals must be perceived as realistic and attainable.

-- Those people with dreams are the ones most likely to experience them.

-- Set goals carefully for you will attain them. This also means if you set none, you will attain that.

-- Goals, when thoughtfully set, can provide strong motivational direction.

-- Clear cut, understandable and realistic objectives leading to the goal help to maintain the sense of realism and the hope of attainment of the goal.

-- Establish measurement criteria to monitor progressive movement toward your goal. Then you will experience progress.

-- Set goals that you will be proud to have achieved, then sense your having completed them.

-- Have a vision that you know is unquestionably right and you will be internally driven to achieve that vision.

-- A goal is "reasonable" when you can see the

entire process needed to get to its attainment.

-- Good planning assists in sensing reasonableness of challenging goals.

-- Use picture goals.

-- Develop an emotional reason why you should attain your goal.

MEIR LIRAZ